# Picnics

## of

## Tuscany

# *Picnics of Tuscany*

## *Italian Country-Style Picnics to Enjoy*
## *At Home or Abroad*

## Craig Pyes

### *Paintings by Camille Corot*

Simon & Schuster

New York   London   Toronto   Sydney   Tokyo   Singapore

SIMON & SCHUSTER
Rockefeller Center
1230 Avenue of the Americas
New York, New York 10020

AN AERO+ASSOCIATES BOOK

Designed by Rita Aero
Map by Cynthia Fitting
Printed in the United States

1   3   5   7   9   10   8   6   4   2

Library of Congress Cataloging-in-Publication Data

Pyes, Craig
Picnics of Tuscany : Italian country-style picnics to enjoy at home or abroad / by Craig Pyes; paintings by Camille Corot
p.   cm.
1. Cookery, Italian. 2. Cookery, Italian — Tuscan style. 3. Picnicking. 4. Tuscany (Italy) — Description and travel. I. Title.
TX723.P95   1994

641.5945'5—dc20                                   93-34448
                                                  CIP
ISBN 0-671-87015-7

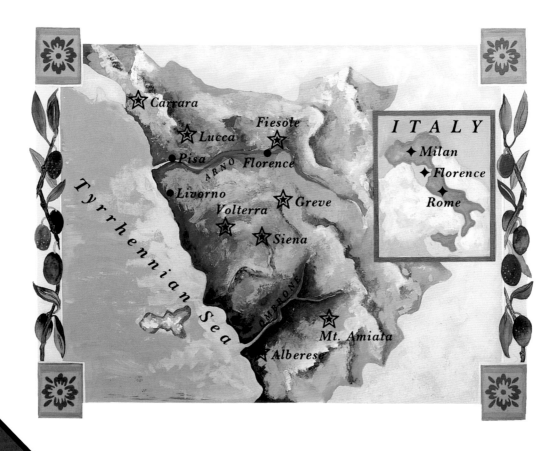

# CONTENTS

~ *28* ~

*Cookout alla Braccia at the Marble Quarries of Carrara*

Bruschetta al Pomodoro *(grilled garlic bread with tomatoes, fresh basil, and olive oil)*

Bistecca alla Fiorentina Gran Pezzo *(grilled T-bone steak Florentine style)*

Fagioli al Fiasco *(white beans cooked in a flask)*

Chianti Classico Riserva *(aged red wine of the region)*

Pere con Pecorino Toscano *(fresh pears with sheeps' milk cheese)*

~ *34* ~

*Lunch Al Fresco Among the Olive Groves at Lucca*

Asparagi all'Agro *(asparagus with olive oil and lemon)*

Vitello Tonnato *(cold veal topped with tuna sauce)*

Insalata Mista *(mixed garden salad)*

Vernaccia di San Gimignano *(white wine of the region)*

Fragoline *(wild strawberries)*

~ *40* ~

*Fattoria Harvest Picnic in the Sienese Countryside*

Crostini Toscani di Fegatini e Vin Santo  *(canapés of chicken liver pâté accompanied with "Holy Wine")*

Panzanella  *(Tuscan bread salad with tomatoes and basil)*

Pollo Arrosto alla Finocchiona  *(cold roasted chicken spiced with fennel seeds)*

Chianti Colli Senesi  *(red wine from Siena)*

Pesche alla Menta con Amaretti  *(peaches in wine spiced with mint and served with bittersweet apricot cookies)*

~ *46* ~

*Seafood Brunch in the Maremma at Alberese*

Prosciutto e Fichi Freschi  *(prosciutto and fresh figs)*

Astice Freddo alla Maniera del Giglio  *(cold lobster bathed in olive oil and lemon)*

Insalata di Scarola al Pecorino e Mela Verde  *(escarole, pecorino cheese, and green apple salad)*

Elba Bianco  *(white wine from the island of Elba)*

Ricotta con Caffè  *(sweetened ricotta cheese with espresso)*

~ 52 ~

*Wine-Tasting Afternoon in the Chianti Countryside at Greve*

Antipasti Misti di Greve  *(hams and salami from Greve)*

Frittata di Carciofi  *(artichoke omelette)*

Pinzimonio  *(fresh vegetables dipped in olive oil)*

Formaggi Misti  *(platter of Italian cheeses)*

Selection of Chiantis  *(a selection of three Chianti wines for tasting)*

~ 58 ~

*Hunters' Autumn Feast in the Foothills of Mt. Amiata*

Insalata di Funghi Porcini  *(wild mushroom salad)*

Quaglie allo Spiedo  *(spit-roasted quail)*

Polenta alla Griglia  *(grilled polenta)*

Morellino di Scansano  *(red wine from Grosetto)*

Castagne di Monte Amiata  *(roasted chestnuts from Mt. Amiata)*

# *An Introduction to Italian Country-Style Picnics*

Italians not only love to eat, they love to eat outdoors. Nowhere is this more apparent than in Tuscany, where a picnic combines the enjoyment of scenic beauty, art, and history with the pleasures of local foods and wines.

Indeed, living and eating well has been a tradition in Tuscany since before the time of the Caesars. Fields that were in cultivation then are still being tilled, and producing vineyards overlay those once tended by the Etruscans, whose paradoxically austere yet sensuous civilization vanished mysteriously before the onslaught of Rome. Today, the inviting Tuscan landscape is little changed from the verdant pastoral scenes of Renaissance Italy portrayed in the paintings of Botticelli, Michelangelo, and da Vinci — Tuscans all. The play of light over the rugged Tuscan landscape and delicate hill towns has drawn artists from all over the world. The paintings in *Picnics of Tuscany* were done by the French artist, Camille Corot, who returned to Italy and Tuscany again and again to portray the beauty of the countryside on canvas. Although not every painting was done in Tuscany, they all capture the mood of the region.

The recipes for this book were assembled largely during a Tuscan autumn, when the sun is intermittent and the subtle, earthy colors of the landscape fade into a chiaroscuro mist. Fall in Tuscany is not always perfect picnic weather, yet groups continue their countryside outings throughout the harvest and feast seasons. Wine grapes are picked, wild mushrooms and chestnuts are gathered, hunters stalk furry and feathery game and, lastly, when the air has chilled, the olives are stripped from the trees.

*Picnics of Tuscany* is designed to transport you and your guests to an authentic Tuscan outing in the heart of Italy's countryside. Each of the eight picnics offers a menu that will re-create the taste and ambience of a different Tuscan locale, for a picnic that can be enjoyed anywhere.

Your gastronomic journey begins with a feast among Renaissance villas on the cypress-clad slopes of Fiesole. You then explore the flavors of ancient Etruria on the commanding windswept plateau of Volterra, which looks out over the Tuscan countryside much as it appeared twenty-five hundred years ago. You join a Tuscan–style barbecue in the marble quarries of Carrara, where Michelangelo chose the stone for his most famous works. On a hot summer day, you can linger over an alfresco lunch in the olive groves of Lucca, enjoy the fruits of the harvest in the Sienese countryside, or stop in Alberese and dine elegantly on lobster from a secluded sea cove in the

Tuscan archipelago. Your picnic journey concludes among the last sunny embers of autumn, with an afternoon of wine tasting in the Chianti region and a rustic hunters' spread in the rugged foothills of Mt. Amiata.

All who take this journey will find Tuscany has much to offer in cooking techniques and fine food: world-class wines and olive oils; fruits and vegetables tenderly grown on small farms; Chianina beef, the best in Italy, transformed into a sizzling *bistecca alla Fiorentina*; abundant wild game; fish from inland waterways; and seafood from the Tyrrhenian Sea.

Unlike formal French cuisine, *la cucina Toscana* foregoes elaborate preparations and sauces for simple, frugal, flavorful cooking. Meats are often spit-roasted or grilled in the traditional country way over wood fires. Stale bread is magically transformed into delicious soups, salads, and desserts. Fresh herbs such as sage, rosemary, and basil impart the savor of the fields, while olive oil spreads its mantle of peppery sweetness.

The recipes, with few exceptions, are traditional Tuscan preparations, many coaxed from the harried chefs and restaurateurs I've met on my travels. The menus include not only picnic fare, but also adaptations of trattoria dishes to make them transportable or easy to prepare out of doors. All the picnics are designed to serve four, so you'll want to shop accordingly for larger or smaller parties.

Always begin your Tuscan picnic at the market. Choose the freshest produce and buy according to season. Use only fresh herbs, never dried. If the ingredients you need are not available at your regular shopping places, look for an Italian specialty store in your area that carries them.

The most essential ingredient of Tuscan cuisine is olive oil. Its transparent veil imparts flavor to a dish, yet allows the natural tastes of food to come through. It is not uncommon to find Tuscan households and restaurants with several varieties on hand to serve with different courses. Delicate recipes call for an olive oil that is somewhat golden in color: light, sweet, and fruity. The darker green olive oils have a more vegetal taste and a scratchy, biting flavor. These can be used in recipes with stronger-tasting ingredients.

The best cold-pressed extra-virgin olive oils are expensive, costing as much, or more, than an expensive bottle of wine — and are worth every penny. The first pressing produces the finest oil, because it has the lowest acid content. To be called extra-virgin *(olio extravergine di oliva),* the oil must contain 1 percent or less of oleic acid. Extra-virgin olive oil from the Chianti region of Tuscany averages about $3/10$ percent, and is generally regarded as among the best in the world. However, just because a bottle is labeled "extra-virgin," it does not ensure a high-quality oil. Inexpensive, mass-produced extra-virgin olive oil can be pale, over-refined, and blended with non-Italian oils.

The key, always, is in the taste. Inexpensive olive oils are perfectly fine for most cooking, but select the very best you can find when it is to be used as a flavoring for salad dressings and vegetables. Store olive oil in a cool, dark place and consume it within a year, since the flavor will deteriorate.

Because Tuscany is one of the world's foremost wine-producing areas, each picnic menu suggests a local wine to accompany the meal. Some of these wines may not be available in your area, so suitable alternatives are listed. You will, of course, need to bring along a *cavatappi* (corkscrew) and wineglasses, but overall, Tuscan picnics call for little equipment: a basket for the utensils and food, and a tablecloth or ground cover for your guests are the basic requirements. You will need sealed containers to transport foods and a sharp knife for cutting meats and bread. You may also wish to pack your basket with *acqua minerale,* which is ubiquitous at Italian picnics. In the summer, it is a good idea to carry perishable ingredients, desserts, and white wines in a cooler. And when serving foods prepared with raw egg, such as the sauce in *vitello tonnato,* take special care to use the freshest eggs and to keep the dish chilled until served.

For each of the Tuscan picnics, I have made suggestions for selecting and preparing your picnic site, along with some ideas for activities before or after the meal. Be inventive — and enjoy this delicious cuisine. *Buon appetito!*

F ive miles north of Florence, the ancient Etruscan hilltop town of Fiesole is celebrated for its sweeping view of the Tuscan countryside. Its slopes are filled with earth-toned villas that seem baked right into the land. Their opulent gardens peer out over rolling hills studded with cypress, oak, and silvery olive groves suffused in the kind of light that inspired the great masterpieces of the Renaissance. Florence and the Val d'Arno shimmer in the haze below, and fields cultivated since antiquity stretch as far as Arezzo.

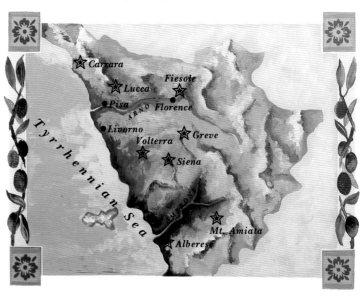

# *Picnic with a View at Fiesole*

Along the curving mountain road to Fiesole, one can find the perfect view overlooking Florence and the surrounding countryside. It was on Fiesole's slopes that Boccaccio set the *Decameron*, and here one can find the familiar Italian landscapes that are depicted in the paintings of the Renaissance masters.

    The slopes are dotted with cypress trees and Renaissance pleasure villas with beautiful gardens and views of the countryside beyond. Just before the sun sets, great platters of food are brought into the gardens and families and friends settle down among the blue violets to enjoy a sumptuous Florentine meal — a noble loin of roast pork, white beans scented with fragrant herbs, and a bottle of Tuscany's best wine.

Insalata di Pignoli, Rugola, e Parmigiano  *(salad with pine nuts, arugula, and Parmesan cheese)*

Arista alla Fiorentina  *(roast loin of pork, Florentine style)*

Fagioli all'Uccelletto  *(white beans cooked "like little birds" with tomatoes, garlic, and sage)*

Brunello di Montalcino  *(fine red wine from Montalcino)*

Pere al Forno con Pignoli  *(baked pears in wine sauce with pine nuts)*

Since this is a perfect picnic to enjoy at sundown, you can prepare the dishes on the morning of the same day. Shop the day before for the meat, cheese, wine, produce, pears, and beans, and soak the beans overnight. On the day of your picnic dinner, pick up a loaf of fresh Italian bread.

*INSALATA DI PIGNOLI, RUGOLA, E PARMIGIANO:* This little salad, which blends slightly bitter arugula with the woody flavor of pine nuts and the tartness of Parmesan cheese, is so simple to make that you almost feel guilty that it tastes so good.

On the morning of your garden picnic, wash and dry about half a pound of arugula, cut away the stems, put in it a bag, and refrigerate. Just before you're ready to serve the meal, cut the arugula into thin strips and place it in a salad bowl. Add one-and-a-half ounces of slivered Parmesan and a generous handful of pine nuts. Toss with about three tablespoons of extra-virgin olive oil until each leaf is lightly coated; add just enough fresh lemon juice for tartness, about one tablespoon, and salt to taste.

*ARISTA ALLA FIORENTINA:* This slowly roasted loin of pork infused with fresh spices is one of Florence's most notable delicacies, and is good served hot or cold. The recipe is adapted from the one used at the well-known Florentine trattoria, Coco Lezzone.

Choose a pork loin roast weighing about three pounds, and prepare it early on the day of your picnic dinner. Cut away the excess fat and clean the meat. Finely chop together two cloves of garlic, a sprig of fresh rosemary (about one-half teaspoon), four fresh sage leaves, salt, and ground

pepper. With a sharp knife, make several deep incisions in the meat and stuff them with the chopped herbs and spices. Coat the outside of the roast with olive oil, and sprinkle with salt and pepper and a bit more of the sage and rosemary. Place the meat in a small roasting pan filled with about an inch of water. Roast uncovered in a preheated 325-degree oven for one to two hours, basting occasionally. The roast is cooked when the juices run clear when the roast is pierced with a fork. Remove the roast to a plate, allow it to cool, then wrap in aluminum foil to keep it moist until you are ready to eat. The meat will be served at room temperature.

*FAGIOLI ALL'UCCELLETTO:* Beans cooked "liked little birds" gets its name from the Tuscan preparation of small game birds with tomatoes and sage.

The night before your picnic, place about three-quarters of a pound of dry white beans in cold water to soak overnight. The next day, rinse the beans, put them in a large pot, and cover them with fresh water, but do not add salt. Simmer the beans for one to two hours, testing them to see if they're tender. Add water as needed. Add salt to taste when the beans are just tender, and continue cooking for about fifteen minutes longer.

Meanwhile, heat three tablespoons of olive oil in a large skillet, and add two cloves of crushed garlic, five chopped fresh sage leaves, and coarsely ground pepper; sauté until the garlic begins to change color. Drain the beans and add them to the hot skillet. Stir in four peeled and chopped large tomatoes (or one large can whole tomatoes, drained and chopped) and simmer the beans for twenty minutes. Taste and add salt if necessary. Like the roast, the beans can be eaten at room temperature.

*BRUNELLO DI MONTALCINO:* This aged, fragrant, full-bodied red from the rolling hills surrounding the picturesque village of Montalcino is one of Italy's finest wines. If you don't have the budget of the Medici, however, a Chianti Classico Riserva or Vino Nobile di Montepulciano are excellent alternatives.

*PERE AL FORNO CON PINGOLI:* Make the pears on the day of your outing. Thinly slice the bottoms off of four large pears, and stand them up close together in a small casserole. Pour in equal amounts of red and white wine to the pears' waist level and add one-fourth cup of sugar and a few slices of orange and lemon peel. Bake the pears at the same preheated temperature as the *arista* (325 degrees) for about one hour. Transfer the fruit to a plate (the pears will retain their shape but look wrinkled), let cool, cover, and refrigerate. Meanwhile, return the casserole to the oven and reduce the sauce until it thickens, then transfer it to a separate container. To serve, cut the pears in half lengthwise, scoop out the cores, and arrange on a platter or individual dessert plates. Pour the syrup over the pear halves and sprinkle them with pine nuts.

## *S t a g i n g   t h e   G a r d e n   P i c n i c*

If you are dining in your own garden with a view, you can simply carry your meal outdoors when the sun is low in the sky. Don't forget the wineglasses and a crisp white tablecloth, for a bottle of Brunello is an occasion, indeed. Start with the salad, then carve the roast and serve it with the beans. Pass around some Italian bread. Let your guests savor the meal and the Brunello as they adjust to the gradually gathering dusk.

W indswept Volterra, perched on a rocky bluff thirty miles from the Tyrrhenian Sea, was the most northerly of the great Etruscan cities. From the plateau's desolate ridges, you can see into the heart of Tuscany and imagine the boundaries of the Confederation of city states of northern Etruria as it was twenty-five hundred years ago. Due east sits Arezzo; along the Val di Chiana stands Cortona, then Chiusi; completing the circle are Vetulonia and Populonia, the maritime cities of the coastal plain, whose Etruscan origins have now all vanished into a labyrinth of tombs.

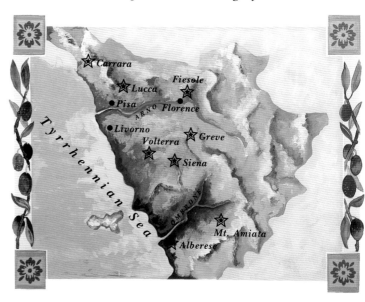

# *Etruscan Banquet*
# *in the Countryside at Volterra*

The Etruscans dominated the whole of Tuscany, their cities of wood crowning the hills. They turned the Etrurian plains into waving fields of wheat, drained the swamps, stocked the rivers and lakes with fish, and exported the wine they produced. Their somber paintings show erotic scenes of sun-darkened men and pale women banqueting alfresco and dancing under the languid eyes of Flufluns, the god of joy and wine.

When not feasting, the Etruscans were obsessed with foretelling the future in the patterns of nature. Perhaps they foretold their own disappearance — saw their wooden temples evaporate, their language dissolve into mystery. What remains today are their stone tombs and delicately crafted artifacts, and their lingering influence on the cuisine of Northern Italy.

Antipasti Misti  *(cheese frittata, prosciutto, melon, and black olives)*

Trota alla Griglia  *(grilled brook trout with rosemary)*

Insalata di Pomodori, Cetrioli, Cipolla, Peperone, e Basilico  *(salad of tomatoes, cucumber, onion, red pepper, and basil)*

Bianco di Pitigliano  *(dry white wine of the region)*

Vin Santo e Biscotti *(dessert wine and dry almond biscuits)*

# *Preparing the Etruscan Banquet*

Shop the day before your picnic for the fresh trout and produce. Stop at an Italian specialty store for the prosciutto, black olives, goat cheese, almond biscuits, and wines. Most foods will be prepared the morning of your picnic; the trout can be cooked at home or grilled at your picnic site. On the way to your picnic, stop at a bakery for a fresh loaf of Italian bread.

*ANTIPASTI MISTI:* This Etruscan repast begins with antipasti — black olives, thin slices of prosciutto di Parma and chilled melon, and wedges of cheese frittata.

Make the two frittatas on the morning of your picnic. Preheat the oven to 375 degrees. In a small bowl lightly beat two eggs with a dash of salt and pepper. Crumble about two ounces of fresh sheep or goat cheese into the eggs. Heat two tablespoons of olive oil in a small ovenproof skillet over medium heat, then pour in the eggs and lower the heat. Cook slowly until the eggs form a crust on the bottom and the top is runny. Place the skillet in the preheated oven for about five minutes, or until the top becomes firm and golden. Loosen the frittata with a spatula, tip it onto a plate, and repeat the entire process for the second frittata. Allow the frittatas to cool, then wrap them separately.

Meanwhile, peel, seed, and thinly slice a small cantaloupe. Reassemble the slices, wrap them tightly, and refrigerate until you are ready to leave. At your picnic site, cut the frittatas into small wedges and arrange them on a large platter along with the black olives and slices of melon wrapped in prosciutto.

*TROTA ALLA GRIGLIA:* The rivers and lakes of ancient Etruria teemed with trout, and one can hardly imagine that these tasty fish were not part of the Etruscan diet. The trout, perfumed with rosemary, can be cooked at home the morning of your picnic or grilled at your picnic site.

Rinse four small trout under cold water and blot them dry. Sprinkle the insides with coarse sea salt and freshly ground pepper, and put a sprig of fresh rosemary inside each fish. Brush the outside of the fish with olive oil.

To broil the trout at home, preheat the broiler, place the rack about four inches from the heat and cook for about five minutes on each side, or until the flesh is opaque throughout. Remove the fish, let them cool to room temperature, then wrap them tightly and pack in your basket.

If you are cooking the trout at your picnic site, use a fragrant wood and/or charcoal for your fire, and let the coals burn down low. Coat the grill with oil so that the fish does not stick, and cook the trout for about three to five minutes on a side, or until the flesh is opaque. Allow the fish to cool slightly in the open air while you serve the antipasti.

When you're ready for the fish, open them flat, remove the rosemary sprigs, and debone. Squeeze a little lemon juice over the trout and drizzle them with extra-virgin olive oil.

*INSALATA DI POMODORI, CETRIOLI, CIPOLLA, PEPERONE, E BASILICO:* This traditional salad with summery ripe tomatoes and fresh basil is a delicious and refreshing accompaniment to the trout. Before you leave for your picnic site, cut a medium red onion in half lengthwise and slice it into very thin half-moons. Soak the slices for twenty minutes in cold water to sweeten them. Meanwhile, fill a picnic container with three vine-ripened tomatoes cut into small wedges; one cucumber peeled and cut in half lengthwise, then sliced into half rounds; and one medium green or red bell pepper cut into thin bite-sized strips. Remove the onion from the water, pat dry, and add to the salad. Seal the container and refrigerate until you're ready to leave. To serve, toss the salad with salt, extra-virgin olive oil, and about one-and-a-half tablespoons of balsamic vinegar.

*BIANCO DI PITIGLIANO:* This pleasantly dry white wine from Grosetto, with a slightly bitter aftertaste, comes from ancient vineyards whose roots reach down to the buried ruins of Etruria. If it is not available, substitute a Vernaccia or any other white wine of Tuscany.

*VIN SANTO E BISCOTTI:* Vin Santo served with *biscotti* (dry almond biscuits) is traditionally offered at the end of a meal in Tuscany. Select a sweet Vin Santo; some varieties can be quite dry. To serve, pour your guests small glasses of Vin Santo and pass a plate of *biscotti* to be dipped in the wine as they are eaten.

## *Staging the Etruscan Banquet*

According to the depiction in their artwork, Etruscan banquets were elegant, open-air affairs, so decorate the table with garlands gathered at your picnic site. Perhaps your guests will bring bowls of fruit — grapes, apricots, and pomegranates (the Etruscan symbol of female fertility). At a proper Etruscan banquet the guests would recline among painted pottery and amphoras of wine. During their festivals and feasts the Etruscans gave themselves to wild abandon with music and dance. Dogs and other pets are usually pictured at play in the frescoes of their festivities, but you may wish to forego the chained cheetahs and lions.

J ust beyond the sandy beaches of the Ligurian Sea, the marble crests and domes of the Apuan Apennines cast their icy glint. Within these mountain folds you come upon Carrara, its industrious streets filled with stone cutters, sculptors, and masons — all powdered with fine white dust. The steep valleys beyond the town are veined with quarries that have provided marble for over two thousand years — from the immense blocks that were used to form the great monuments of the Roman Empire, to the pieces that became the subtle and moving sculptures of the Renaissance.

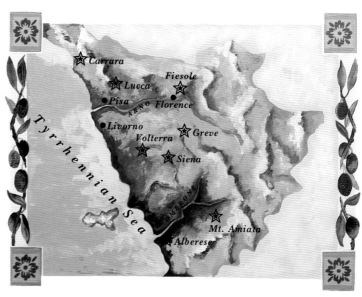

# *Cookout alla Braccia at the Marble Quarries of Carrara*

Carrara's bounty is rock — crystallized limestone that over time has been pressed into white marble prized for its purity and fine grain. The quarries — more than three hundred of them — are as stark and angular as a cubist's dream. For centuries sculptors such as Michelangelo have traveled here to supervise the cutting and shaping of the rock, in order to release the forms and images imprisoned inside.

Sculptors, architects, and casual visitors ramble through the stony glens, passing from shadeless light to cold darkness seeking the perfect stone. After a day of quarry hiking, dinner is celebrated out of doors with a Tuscan-style barbecue, and everyone pitches in to cook thick, tender Chianina beefsteaks *alla braccia*.

Bruschetta al Pomodoro  *(grilled garlic bread with tomatoes, fresh basil, and olive oil)*

Bistecca alla Fiorentina Gran Pezzo  *(grilled T-bone steak Florentine style)*

Fagioli al Fiasco  *(white beans cooked in a flask)*

Chianti Classico Riserva  *(aged red wine of the region)*

Pere con Pecorino Toscano  *(fresh pears with sheeps' milk cheese)*

## *Preparing the Carrara Cookout*

Shop the day before the picnic for the steaks, beans, fruit, produce, cheese, and wine. You can prepare the beans at home, or you can cook them at the barbecue site if you begin at least three hours before you plan to eat. On the way to your picnic site, stop at the bakery for a loaf of crusty country-style bread.

*BRUSCHETTA AL POMODORO:* This garlic bread grilled over charcoal is an excellent first course, and should be eaten hot off the grill. Without the tomatoes and basil it is called *fett'unta.*

At your picnic site, cut six small plum tomatoes into half-inch cubes, and slice a handful of fresh basil into thin strips. Meanwhile, grill four large, thick slices of country-style bread on both sides until brown. Remove the toasted bread, rub one side of each slice vigorously with a cut garlic clove, and drizzle on a little extra-virgin olive oil. Top the slices with the chopped tomato, strips of fresh basil, a dash of sea salt, and another drizzle of olive oil. Serve immediately.

*BISTECCA ALLA FIORENTINA:* Florence gave birth not only to the Renaissance, but to a grilled steak that has become its best-known dish. The cut of meat, which resembles an American T-bone, comes from young Chianina beef, the white humpbacked cattle that graze on the hills of Arezzo. Florentine steaks cook best when they are large enough for two people, so choose two T-bones that are at least one-and-three-quarters pounds each.

At your picnic site, prepare a plate of olive oil and coarsely ground black pepper. When the coals are very hot, turn the meat in the peppered olive oil to coat both sides and place on the grill.

Cook the steak seven minutes on each side, turning once, for medium rare. Neither meat nor heat is ever uniform, so check the steaks several times until they're cooked the way you like them. When done, put the steaks on a large platter, sprinkle with salt, and serve sizzling.

*FAGIOLI AL FIASCO:* Beans cooked in a bottle is a traditional Tuscan dish, and the cooking process must begin long before you've worked up an appetite. The traditional cooking vessel is a large (one-and-a-half liters) pear-shaped Chianti bottle with the straw removed. About three-quarters of a pound of small white Tuscan beans or *cannellini* are poured into the bottle along with three tablespoons of extra-virgin olive oil and two crushed large garlic cloves. The bottle is filled with cold water, plugged with straw or cloth to let the steam escape, and placed close to an open fire so that the beans can simmer constantly for three to four hours until the water and oil have been absorbed.

The beans may be prepared at home with much less fuss and time. The night before your picnic, place the beans in a large pot and soak them overnight in cold water. The next morning, pour off the water, rinse the beans, and cover them again with fresh water. Simmer the beans for one to two hours, adding water as needed. After about one hour, add two large crushed garlic cloves and three tablespoons of olive oil to the pot and continue simmering. When the beans are just tender, add salt to taste and cook fifteen minutes longer.

Allow the beans to cool until you are ready to leave for your picnic. Transport them in a container that can be heated near the coals. When you are ready to eat, spoon the beans into individual bowls, drizzle with extra-virgin olive oil, and add freshly cracked pepper.

*CHIANTI CLASSICO RISERVA:* Chianti Classico Riserva has been aged in oak at least three years. The wine has a garnet color, and emerges with plenty of structure and tannins to cleanse the palate and enhance the flavor of your steak.

*PERE CON PECORINO TOSCANO:* This sharp, slightly crumbly sheeps' milk cheese comes in dozens of shapes and varieties, but it is most commonly exported as romano. The "bite" of the cheese, when aged, enhances the flavor of the sweet, cool pears, which are a traditional finish to a country meal.

## Staging the Carrara Cookout

This hearty, playful picnic can take the edge off of the most difficult work week. Choose a picnic site with cooking facilities, somewhere with natural surroundings that cast cool shadows in the late afternoon — a rocky cliff or a stand of tall trees. Start your fire early in the day, using fragrant wood and/or charcoal to impart flavor to the meat. Put the *fagioli al fiasco* nearby to warm. While the coals burn down, bring out a box of twine, wire, hammer, and nails, and challenge your guests to create sculptures from found objects in the area. Or you could bring along sculpting clay for your guests. Who knows — one of them may become the next Michelangelo?

Start your cookout when the coals are hot and the shadows long. Open the wine and toast your masterpieces, then let everyone make their own *bruschetta* and eat it as the steaks sizzle and hiss on the grill. When the steaks are done, put them on platters big enough for two, and serve small bowls of beans drenched in olive oil.

W edged between the Gulf of Genoa to the west, and the steep, rugged hills of Garfagnana to the north, the walled city of Lucca is famed for the quality of its olive oil. In the summer, the olive tree-clad hills beyond the city offer a delicate, shaded canopy of escape from the fierce sun. In the chill of autumn, when the grapes have been picked and the vines have turned to yellow and rust, the groves will again fill with people to collect the tart, green fruit from the trees and turn it into liquid gold.

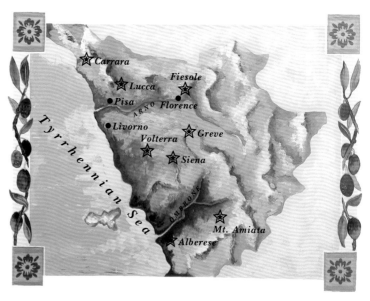

# Lunch Al Fresco Among the Olive Groves at Lucca

Outside the imposing walls of Lucca, past country villas and open parks, olive groves and vineyards cling to the hillsides. On hot summer days, olive leaves flash metallically above gnarled boughs as picnickers lunch in the shade underneath to escape the heat.

When the olive season starts in November, women in voluminous floral skirts lodge themselves in the trees like giant fowl. With olive baskets strapped to their waists and nets spread beneath them, their experienced hands strip the twigs bare of the ripening fruit. The leaves whistle through their palms, and the olives they miss pelt the ground in a gentle rain. At the *frantoio* — the olive press — the olives are crushed, then pressed, while the gatherers sit by an open fire drinking wine and munching grilled toast drizzled with the fresh-pressed, peppery oil.

Asparagi all'Agro  *(asparagus with olive oil and lemon)*

Vitello Tonnato  *(cold veal topped with tuna sauce)*

Insalata Mista  *(mixed garden salad)*

Vernaccia di San Gimignano  *(white wine of the region)*

Fragoline  *(wild strawberries)*

Rather than a picnic basket, bring an ice-filled cooler for this cool summer meal. Shop the day before for the veal, asparagus, greens, strawberries, and other produce you will need. Stop at an Italian specialty store for the tuna, wine, and extra-virgin olive oil. The veal and asparagus may be prepared ahead, so only simple preparations will be required on the morning of this indulgent outing. On the way to your picnic site, stop at the bakery for fresh bread sticks or an Italian loaf.

*ASPARAGI ALL'AGRO:* In Italy, this dish is eaten hot during the fall and served cold at summer picnics. The asparagus is precooked, then "anointed" with delicious extra-virgin olive oil and fresh lemon juice just before it is served.

On the morning of your picnic, cut the tough ends off of about one-and-a-half pounds of large asparagus. If the skin is tough, peel the asparagus, then tie them into one or two bunches. Place the bunches upright in a tall pot filled with about three inches of cold salted water. Cover the asparagus and steam them for about six minutes, or until the spears are just al dente. Untie the bunches and plunge the asparagus into cold water to stop the cooking. Drain and wrap the asparagus and pack it in your cooler.

To serve, lay the asparagus on a plate and sprinkle with olive oil and the juice of one lemon. Add salt and freshly ground pepper to taste.

*VITELLO TONNATO:* While cold veal topped with tuna sauce is not a traditional Tuscan dish, it has been locally adopted as a favorite choice for a light summer lunch.

On the day before your picnic, select a two- to three-pound veal roast. Trim off the excess fat and place the roast in a pot with just enough water to cover it. Salt the water and surround the roast with one peeled and quartered onion, and pieces of two celery stalks and one carrot. Cover the pot and let the veal simmer for one hour, then let it cool in its juices. Remove the meat, discard the vegetables, wrap the meat, and refrigerate it overnight.

Make the *tonnato* sauce on the morning of your picnic. Allow the ingredients to warm to room temperature before you begin. Whisk two egg yolks and a pinch of salt in a warm bowl until fluffy. Add a few drops of olive oil and whisk until it is absorbed by the egg yolks. Continue adding the oil (about three quarters of a cup) a little at a time, whisking continually until the mixture emulsifies and thickens. When all the oil has been absorbed, whisk in the juice of one lemon. Drain and mash a small tin of Italian oil-packed tuna (four to six ounces) and add it to the mixture along with one tablespoon of capers. Blend the ingredients well, taste, and add salt if needed. Place the mixture in a covered container and pack it in your picnic cooler.

To serve the veal, slice it as thinly as possible and arrange the slices on a platter. Put a dollop of *tonnato* on each slice and decorate the platter with lemon wedges and watercress.

*INSALATA MISTA:* A summer salad should be a vegetable bouquet, so select from a variety of greens: chicory, escarole, romaine, and arugula. On the morning of your picnic, wash, dry, and tear the greens into bite-sized pieces and put them in a picnic bowl. Clean, quarter, and thinly slice one fennel bulb; cut two medium carrots into small rounds; and cut one red bell pepper into strips. Add the cut vegetables to the salad bowl and pack it in your picnic cooler. Just before you serve the *insalata mista*, slice in two plum tomatoes, add a pinch of salt, and toss with just enough olive oil to make the leaves glisten. Add a very light touch of wine or balsamic vinegar and toss again.

*VERNACCIA DI SAN GIMIGNANO:* This pale, straw-colored wine, grown under the medieval towers of San Gimignano, is one of the oldest and most lauded wines of Tuscany. Poets have sung its praises, popes have bathed in it — and you can drink it with *vitello tonnato,* too. Serve the Vernaccia chilled.

*FRAGOLINE:* Both wild and cultivated strawberries begin appearing in spring, and are a sweet refreshing finish to a summer meal. The small, wild wood strawberries, if you can find them, are eaten plain for their delicate, ambrosial taste. If you're using cultivated strawberries, wash and hull two baskets of strawberries and cut them into quarters on the morning of your picnic; refrigerate them in a picnic bowl. Just before you leave, sprinkle the strawberries with the juice of one lemon and a little sugar; they will marinate in the picnic cooler until you're ready for dessert.

## *S t a g i n g   t h e   L u n c h   A l   F r e s c o*

You are lying under the olive boughs and as happy as the grass is green. The silvery leaves quiver in the breeze and butterflies float carelessly about — the ideal setting for a picnic. Why not bring crystal bowls for the salad and strawberries to show off their vibrant colors? And while you're at it, you may as well serve the asparagus and veal on silver platters, and place the entire feast on an immaculate white linen tablecloth. Let the Vernaccia repose on ice, its golden neck glistening in the sun. A vase filled with just-picked wildflowers is the perfect centerpiece. *Salute.*

The city of Siena, a bowl of burnt red brick around a conch-shaped piazza, is where the Middle Ages meets the Renaissance. To the north and west, the medieval castles of the Sienese Chianti and the fortified walls spiked with menacingly beautiful towers at Monteriggioni and San Gimignano reveal a history of constant strife. To the south you see evidence of a more peaceful time — graceful Renaissance palaces in Montalcino, Pienza, and Montepulciano look out over pastures redolent with herbs and wildflowers, and vineyards that produce world-famous wines.

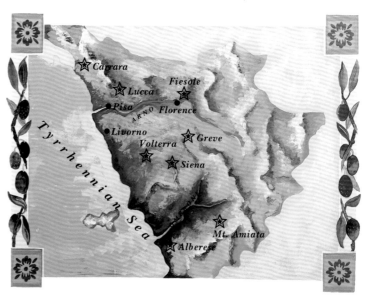

# *Fattoria Harvest Picnic in the Sienese Countryside*

The Sienese countryside is a patchwork of fields flowing between hillside towns. The hot sun peeks between the clouds, the corn — pale green and golden — is plump on the stalks, and rivers of scarlet poppies cascade down hillsides and fill the roadside ditches. The *contadini* (farmers) and city folk work side by side to collect the summer harvest, their overalls stained from the fields.

Every half hour, the workers gather in the shade for small glasses of chilled Vin Santo. When the sun reaches its zenith, work stops for a leisurely outdoor meal. Heaping platters arrive — roasted fowl spiced with fennel seeds, a salad made from the sweet tomatoes and basil collected in the fields, and wine sent over from the neighboring vineyards.

Crostini Toscani di Fegatini e Vin Santo  *(canapés of chicken liver pâté accompanied with "Holy Wine")*

Panzanella  *(Tuscan bread salad with tomatoes and basil)*

Pollo Arrosto alla Finocchiona  *(cold roasted chicken spiced with fennel seeds)*

Chianti Colli Senesi  *(red wine from Siena)*

Pesche alla Menta con Amaretti  *(peaches in wine spiced with mint and served with bittersweet apricot cookies)*

# *Preparing the Harvest Picnic*

Shop the day before your picnic for the chicken, fruit, and vegetables, and purchase bottles of Sienese Chianti and sweet Vin Santo. At the bakery, pick up a baguette, the *amaretti*, and a loaf of hearty Italian country-style bread for the salad; day-old bread is ideal, since it should be stale. Except for the salad, most of the dishes can be prepared the day before your picnic.

*CROSTINI TOSCANI DI FEGATINI ET VIN SANTO: Crostini*, an Italian version of canapés, are served as an antipasto throughout Tuscany. The little toasts play host to a wide variety of toppings, but chicken liver pâté is the local favorite.

Prepare the pâté the day before your picnic. Melt two tablespoons of butter in a skillet over medium heat, and sauté one finely chopped onion until it becomes translucent. Add six chicken livers and sauté for five minutes, until the outsides brown but the insides are still pink. With a fork, break the livers into small chunks and add about one-half cup of dry white wine; lower the heat and simmer to evaporate the liquid slowly. As the livers cook, add one tablespoon of capers and one teaspoon of anchovy paste, and mash everything into a paste. To keep the pâté creamy as it cooks, add chicken stock one tablespoon at a time. Salt and pepper to taste and cook for ten minutes more, then transfer to a heatproof picnic bowl, cover, and refrigerate overnight.

On the morning of your picnic, slice a baguette into thin rounds and toast them. Wrap the toasts in paper and pack them in your picnic basket along with the pâté. At your picnic site, brush the toasts with olive oil, spread with pâté, and sprinkle fresh chopped parsley over the tops.

Serve the *crostini* as a first course accompanied with small glasses of chilled sweet Vin Santo, Tuscany's famous dessert wine.

***PANZANELLA:*** This delicious summer salad owes its success to the rustic, peasant-inspired marriage of stale bread and crisp, fresh garden vegetables. On the morning of your picnic, cut six thick slices from a hearty Italian country-style loaf that has been left out to harden. Soak the slices in cold water until they soften. Meanwhile, coarsely chop three vine-ripened tomatoes, one peeled cucumber, one Bermuda onion, and two stalks of celery. Put the chopped vegetables in a picnic bowl. Remove the softened bread from the water, squeeze out as much of the water as possible, crumble or tear the bread into pieces, and add to the chopped vegetable salad. Add about ten finely shredded fresh basil leaves, and salt and pepper to taste. Dress the salad liberally with extra-virgin olive oil and toss. Refrigerate the *panzanella* for about two hours, or until you are ready to leave. At your picnic site, sprinkle the salad with a little red wine vinegar to taste.

***POLLO ARROSTO ALLA FINOCCHIONA:*** Roasted chicken spiced with fennel seeds was a favored recipe in ancient Rome. Although this roasted chicken is also delicious served hot, the fennel seeds add a refreshing note when the dish is eaten cold on a summer afternoon.

On the day before your outing, select a three-pound free-range chicken. Sprinkle the inside of the chicken with salt, pepper, and about one tablespoon of fennel seeds. Truss the chicken with cotton string and place it in a roasting pan. Rub the skin with olive oil and sprinkle with salt, pepper, and more fennel seeds.

In a preheated 425-degree oven, cook the chicken for fifteen minutes to brown the skin and seal in the juices, then reduce the heat to 350 degrees and continue roasting for another forty-five minutes, basting frequently with the juices in the pan. When the chicken is done, remove it from the oven and let it cool to room temperature, then wrap it tightly and refrigerate overnight.

*CHIANTI COLLI SENESI:* This pleasant, light Chianti from the Sienese hills comes from the Colli Senesi vineyards, which border most of the major wine-growing regions in the province. Chianti Colli Senesi is an excellent choice with poultry. Serve slightly chilled.

*PESCHE ALLA MENTA CON AMARETTI:* This dessert may be prepared the evening before your picnic or early that morning. Blanch four large ripe peaches (or eight small ones) in boiling water for two minutes. Remove the peaches and skin them but leave them whole. In a bowl, dissolve two tablespoons of sugar in one cup of dry white wine and add several sprigs of mint. Put the peaches in the bowl and add enough wine to cover them. Cover the bowl and marinate for several hours or overnight in the refrigerator. Serve the chilled peaches in dessert bowls with a little of the marinade and fresh sprigs of mint, and pass around a plate of crunchy amaretti cookies.

## *Staging the Harvest Picnic*

In the summer, the fields begin to vibrate with the energy of nature and draw everyone to the countryside. It is natural, therefore, for Tuscans to participate in the harvest — not only the *contadini*, but city folk as well. Many farms allow passersby to pick produce to take home. Why not spend the morning of your outing with some friends in the orchards or fields? Afterward, open the chilled Vin Santo, and pour everyone a small glass to launch your harvest picnic.

The Maremma is a one-hundred-mile strip of marsh and thicket along the Grosetto coast. The shore is dotted with hidden coves, sandy white beaches, and small fishing villages with boat-filled harbors. The tiny town of Alberese, on the outskirts of Monti dell'Uccellina nature park, is home to wild boar, roebuck, and migrating birds. Along the marshes, mounted butteri — Italian cowboys — guide herds of cattle, their distant figures silhouetted against the sun as it disappears behind the little islands of the Tuscan archipelago spangling in the Tyrrhenian Sea.

46

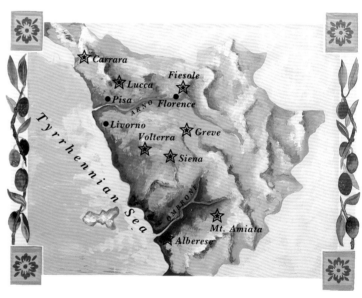

# *Seafood Brunch in the Maremma at Alberese*

The fertile coastal plain of the Maremma, Tuscany's Wild West, was more densely populated in Etruscan times than now. From the Middle Ages until the twentieth century, when reclamation efforts began, the area was known chiefly as a malaria-infested moorland, a place of danger and threats. Brigands hid out in the marshes, Saracen pirates fed on the rich sea trade, and Spanish galleons patrolled from garrisoned ports.

Today the Maremma is home to nature reserves, rich agriculture, and rodeos by the sea at Alberese. It is also the place to find some of the best cooking in Tuscany. The *tipica cucina* of Maremma is simple and rustic, drawing equally on seafood from the Tyrrhenian Sea, freshwater fish from the rivers and lagoons, and wild game that roam the coastal hills and marshes.

Prosciutto e Fichi Freschi  *(prosciutto and fresh figs)*

Astice Freddo alla Maniera del Giglio  *(cold lobster bathed in olive oil and lemon)*

Insalata di Scarola al Pecorino e Mela Verde  *(escarole, pecorino cheese, and green apple salad)*

Elba Bianco  *(white wine from the island of Elba)*

Ricotta con Caffè  *(sweetened ricotta cheese with espresso)*

# Preparing the Seafood Brunch

Shop the day before your picnic for the lobster, figs, escarole, and other produce. Stop at an Italian specialty store for the pecorino cheese, ricotta, prosciutto, wine, and chocolate-covered espresso beans. On the way to your picnic site, stop at a bakery to pick up a loaf of Italian bread, and drop by the coffee store to fill your Thermos with espresso.

*PROSCIUTTO E FICHI FRESCHI:* This antipasto, which blends the sweetness of Mediterranean figs with salty Italian ham, is curiously evocative of the sea. Pack twelve ripe figs and twelve thin slices of prosciutto in your picnic basket. At your picnic site, wrap each fig in a thin slice of prosciutto. Arrange the rolled figs on a plate, and see if you can find a local blossom or sprig nearby to decorate the center.

*ASTICE FREDDO ALLA MANIERA DEL GIGLIO:* Although lobster is not considered a Tuscan dish, the prodigious food journalist, Waverly Root, found it to be a specialty of the island of Giglio, where it is served cold, bathed in olive oil, and sprinkled with freshly ground pepper.

Select two freshly cooked two-pound lobsters at a seafood shop. Check to see if the tails are springy and the smell is fresh. A cooked lobster will keep two days in the refrigerator when properly wrapped. If you prefer to purchase live lobster, cook them in salted water the day before your picnic. Clean them, wrap them tightly in plastic wrap, and refrigerate overnight.

At your picnic site, crack the claws to break the shell and expose the meat, and serve the lobster cold. Give each guest a saucer filled with extra-virgin olive oil, a squeeze of fresh lemon juice,

and a sprinkling of salt and freshly ground pepper. Let your guests pick out the meat and dip it in the olive oil as they eat.

*INSALATA DI SCAROLA AL PECORINO E MELA VERDE:* This delightfully simple salad contrasts the slightly bitter escarole with the delicate sweetness of green apple and the sharp bite of aged pecorino. On the morning of your outing, wash a half-pound of Italian escarole (or substitute any other bitter green such as radicchio or curly endive), cut or tear into bite-sized pieces, and place in a picnic bowl. Select an aged pecorino cheese such as romano, and use a cheese knife to shave about one-and-a-half ounces into thin slivers. Add the slivered cheese to the escarole, seal the picnic container, and refrigerate until you are ready to leave.

Finish the salad at your picnic site. Peel and core a tart green apple, then cut it lengthwise, slice it into thin half-moons, and add the apple slices to the salad bowl. Dress the salad with extra-virgin olive oil until the leaves are lightly coated, then toss with one tablespoon of balsamic vinegar, and salt and pepper to taste.

*ELBA BIANCO:* This unique dry white wine from the rocky island of Elba is cultivated to be enjoyed with the harvest from the sea. If it is unavailable, substitute a white Chianti, such as Val d'Arbia, or a white Tuscan wine made from the Trebbiano grape. Or, you can select an Orvieto, a more commercially available cousin from neighboring Umbria. Orvieto is made with Trebbiano Toscano and Malvasia Toscana grapes.

*RICOTTA CON CAFFÈ:* Soft, creamy, fresh ricotta cheese is used often in Maremman desserts. This recipe — variations of which are found throughout Italy — is especially suited for brunch.

Keep the ricotta chilled during your picnic and prepare the dessert at your picnic site.

Just before you leave for your picnic, fill a Thermos with about three cups of hot espresso. If you cannot make espresso at home, stop at a coffee store on the way and purchase four double espressos to fill your Thermos.

At your picnic site, put fourteen ounces of fresh ricotta cheese in a bowl and add about one demitasse-full of espresso and six teaspoons of sugar. Mix well, taste, and adjust for sweetness and flavor. Spoon the ricotta into dessert bowls, lightly dust with unsweetened cocoa, and crown each serving with a chocolate-covered espresso bean. After dessert, serve the hot espresso in demitasse cups and pass around the rest of the chocolate espresso beans.

## *Staging the Seafood Brunch*

The flavors of this elegant morning picnic are sweet and refreshing, like a cool sea breeze from a fresh cove not yet scourged by the sun. At your waterside outing, you may be wearing windbreakers and sun block, but the prosciutto and figs and succulent lobster washed down with cool, crisp Tuscan wine will make you feel as though you were on the verandah of a luxurious Italian seaside resort.

After the meal, why not pursue the activities of your Maremma counterparts — hiking the nature trails, bird-watching in the reserves, horseback riding along the wild coastal plain, canoeing down the Ombrone River, fishing or sailing off the Grosetto coast, or searching for buried treasure in secluded pirate coves.

The via Chiantigiana is one of the most beautiful rural roads in the world, meandering through hills and valleys as it laces together the Florentine and Sienese wine country, once the scene of violent clashes among the medieval barons of the Chianti League. On your way to Greve, or meandering through Gaiole and Radda, you pass castle ramparts rising above the thick, misty woods, ancient abbeys with olive groves and vineyards hugging the hillsides, and tawny stone fattorie, where you can stop and sample wine, olive oil, and honey.

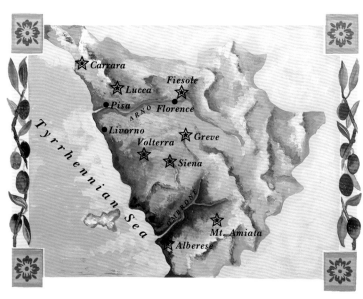

# *Wine-Tasting Afternoon in the Chianti Countryside at Greve*

The Chianti region is at the center of Tuscany. This area of gently rolling hills lies between Siena and Florence, and is staked with signs of the *gallo nero*, the black rooster that symbolizes the vineyards of Chianti Classico in the heart of Chianti's seven wine production zones. Narrow dirt roads veer off the main route past centuries-old farmhouses to elegant villa wineries surrounded by olive groves and vineyards.

In the tasting rooms, bottles are opened, ruby wine is swirled in glasses, and vintages are sipped. Afterwards, when the autumn sun has burned off the mist, the tasters gather in the winery's elegant Renaissance gardens and settle among cypress hedges and trickling fountains to enjoy a simple outdoor meal.

Antipasti Misti di Greve  *(hams and salamis from Greve)*

Frittata di Carciofi  *(artichoke omelette)*

Pinzimonio  *(fresh vegetables dipped in olive oil)*

Formaggi Misti  *(platter of Italian cheeses)*

Selection of Chiantis  *(a selection of three Chianti wines for tasting)*

When people in Tuscany go on a picnic, it is seldom elaborate — which makes this perhaps the most authentic Tuscan picnic in the book. Shop the day before your picnic for the fresh produce you will need, and stop at an Italian specialty store for the meats, cheeses, Tuscan olive oil, and wines. Only the frittata will need to be prepared ahead. On the way to your picnic site, stop at the bakery for a fresh loaf of Italian bread — and don't forget the wineglasses and a corkscrew.

***ANTIPASTI MISTI DI GREVE:*** Virtually every area of Italy produces its own salami, and Tuscany is no exception. In Greve, the main market town of the Chianti, you can find *finocchiona sbriciolona*, a pork salami flavored with fennel seeds; *salami di cinghiale*, made from wild boar; and *prosciutto di Toscano*, a salt-cured ham.

If these salamis are difficult to find, select from locally available Italian salamis; look for one made of pork seasoned with black pepper or fennel. Any good Italian prosciutto will do. Purchase enough meat to cover two small plates, about one-quarter pound of each, and have it sliced very thin. This simple course is a traditional starter for many Tuscan meals.

***FRITTATA DI CARCIOFI:*** Make this Italian omelette on the morning of your picnic. Remove the protruding stem and all the tough outer leaves from eight baby artichokes. When only the tender inner leaves remain, cut the artichokes lengthwise into thin slices and soak them for fifteen minutes in a bowl of water with a squeeze of lemon juice to prevent discoloration. Then remove them and pat dry.

Preheat the oven to 375 degrees. In a bowl, lightly beat eight eggs, adding salt and pepper to taste. In a medium-sized ovenproof skillet, sauté the artichoke slices in three tablespoons of olive oil until they are lightly browned. Reduce the heat and pour the eggs over the artichokes. Cook the eggs slowly until a crust forms on the bottom and only the top is runny. Place the skillet in the oven for about five minutes, or until the omelette becomes firm and golden. Loosen the frittata with a spatula and tip it onto a plate. Let it cool to room temperature, then wrap it and put it in your picnic basket. Serve the frittata in wedges, with freshly chopped parsley sprinkled over the top.

*PINZIMONIO:* In the Chianti, the olive trees and grapevines profit from the same soil and climate, and a few wineries produce and export both wine and olive oil. Emunuela Stucchi Prinetti of Badia a Coltibuono, a wine and olive oil estate located in a former eleventh-century Benedictine monastery near Gaiole, turns her picnics into an olive-oil tasting. She brings fresh vegetables to dip into her own olive oil, to which is added a little salt and pepper.

On the morning of your picnic, wash and cut the following into generous strips: red bell peppers, baby zucchini, fennel, carrots, and celery. Wrap the vegetables tightly and refrigerate until you are ready to leave. Pack a small bottle of high-quality extra-virgin olive oil, preferably from Tuscany. To serve, arrange the vegetables on a platter and give each guest a small dipping bowl to hold olive oil sprinkled with salt and pepper.

*FORMAGGI MISTI:* Italian cheeses are the perfect complement to a wine tasting. Select three cheeses, a mix of aged and fresh; for example, a Gorgonzola, a pecorino, and a provolone.

At your picnic site, arrange the cheeses on a platter, accompanied with a loaf of freshly-baked Italian bread.

*CHIANTIS:* Shop for the wines at a store with a good selection of Italian wines. Chose three different bottles or half bottles from Chianti; at least one should be a Chianti Classico from the original Chianti territory between Chianti Classico bears the mark of the black rooster and has a minimum alcohol content of 12 percent. Select the other wines from outside the Classico area. These wines are produced in six Chianti subzones: Montalbano, Rufina, Colli Fiorentini, Colli Senesi, Colli Aretini, and Colline Pisane. One of your three choices should be a Riserva, wine that has been aged at least three years. A typical selection might include a young Chianti (last year's vintage), Chianti Rufina, and Chianti Classico Riserva.

## *Staging the Chianti Wine Tasting*

Begin your wine tasting when you arrive at your picnic site. Open all the bottles to let the wines breathe. Start with the youngest and least alcoholic of the wines and progress to the oldest and strongest. To taste the wine, pour a small amount into a glass, swirl it around, observe its clarity and color, and sniff its aroma. Taste it slowly, one sip at a time, to appreciate the shadings of flavor. Chiantis are ruby red, dry, and slightly tannic, becoming deeper and smoother as they age. Although you may not be in the Chianti, you should be able to taste the soil, the fruit, and the climate in each bottle of wine. Between each tasting, nibble a piece of bread to cleanse your palate. After you've tasted each wine, put out the platters of food and sample all the wines again.

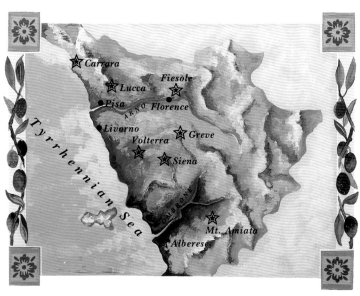

**G**rosetto, Tuscany's southernmost and largest province, abuts the sea, then pushes inland over hills and ridges teeming with game. You begin in the marshy coastal plain of the Maremma, where narrow roads twist through green hills dotted with sheep, then climb steeply into the dense, mushroom-carpeted woods of Monte Amiata. The slopes of this dormant volcano steam with geysers; the sun wheels in and out of clouds; and boar, deer, pheasant, and quail rustle in the thickets among trees that disappear into a veil of mist.

# Hunters' Autumn Feast in the Foothills of Mt. Amiata

The heavy, salt-laden air of the coast turns sharp with the scents of pine and sulfur in the hill country around Saturnia. Here, hot sulfuric rivers course underground from Monte Amiata to feed natural thermal springs that were used before the rise of Rome. Moving inland past waves of grassy hills punctuated by lonely farmhouses and oak and chestnut trees, the woods near Sovana conceal Etruscan burial sites that have weathered centuries of wind and rain.

Farther up, hunters stalking wild game pause for their midday meal, as their dogs busily shake dew from their fur. The hunters carry strings of quail and sacks of a slower game: pale wild mushrooms discovered in the nearby pine forest. They spend a moment examining the luck of the hunt, then begin to build a fire from fragrant wood to cook their lunch.

Insalata di Funghi Porcini  *(wild mushroom salad)*

Quaglie allo Spiedo  *(spit-roasted quail)*

Polenta alla Griglia  *(grilled polenta)*

Morellino di Scansano  *(red wine from Grosetto)*

Castagne di Monte Amiata  *(roasted chestnuts from Mt. Amiata)*

# Preparing the Hunters' Feast

The day before your picnic, purchase the quail, which are sold at specialty butchers. Also pick up the mushrooms, chestnuts, cornmeal, olive oil, wine, and condiments you will need. You will make the olive oil marinade for the quail and prepare the polenta a day in advance. Find a long, thin metal rod to use as a spit to roast the quail. On the morning of your picnic, stop at the bakery for a loaf of crusty Italian bread.

*INSALATA DI FUNGHI PORCINI: Boletus edulis,* the wild porcini mushroom the French know as the *cèpe,* first appears in the hot, wet, waning days of August. Its combination of moist, delicate flesh and woodsy taste make it a delicious salad ingredient. If fresh porcini are unavailable, you may substitute common white mushrooms.

Prepare the salad on the morning of your picnic. Clean one pound of mushrooms by rubbing them with a damp cloth. Cut off the rough stem tips and slice the mushrooms lengthwise as thinly as possible. Place the slices in a large picnic bowl. Toss with two tablespoons of minced fresh parsley and one minced garlic clove. Cover and refrigerate until you are ready to leave. Dress the salad when you just arrive at your picnic site so it can marinate an hour or so before serving. Coat the mushrooms with extra-virgin olive oil, then sprinkle on just enough fresh lemon juice to impart a tang (about half a lemon).

*QUAGLIE ALLO SPIEDO:* Small birds, such as thrush, woodcocks, and partridges, are all fair game during the Tuscan hunting season, but for an impromptu outing, quail is more accessible,

since it is sold commercially. The small birds have a mild, delicate taste, and are traditionally cooked on a spit. The day before your picnic, crush five juniper berries and two cloves of garlic and let them soak overnight in one-half cup of olive oil. Pack this marinade in your picnic basket.

At your picnic site, brush eight quail with the fragrant oil and season them with salt and pepper inside and out. Thread them together on a long metal skewer, and roast them slowly over hot coals, turning them frequently and basting them with the remaining oil. Roast them for fifteen to twenty minutes, or until the outsides are golden brown and the flesh is firm. The quail are served with grilled polenta.

*POLENTA ALLA GRIGLIA:* Polenta is made from coarsely ground cornmeal, and can be served as thick porridge or left to cool into a cake. The day before your picnic, bring three cups of salted water to a boil in a heavy pot. Mix one cup of polenta (or coarsely ground yellow cornmeal) with one cup of cold water and add the mixture to the boiling water. Stir constantly with a wooden spoon to prevent lumping. Lower the heat to simmer, and continue to stir until the mixture becomes the consistency of very thick porridge. Cook for about thirty minutes, stirring frequently, or until the mixture becomes creamy and tender, and pulls away from the sides of the pot. Fill a small baking dish to the top with the hot polenta. Let it cool and refrigerate overnight. Before you leave, remove the polenta cake, wrap it, and pack it in your basket.

When the quail is done, cut the polenta into eight slices, brush the slices with olive oil, and place them on a hot grill for a few minutes. Turn them so they become crispy on both sides, and serve along with the quail.

***MORELLINO DI SCANSANO:*** This balmy red wine is produced in the abandoned Etruscan vineyards of the Maremman hills above Grosetto. It is reminiscent of a light Chianti, but more ethereal and fragrant. The wine is surprisingly versatile, and makes an excellent accompaniment to game birds. If you have trouble locating it, a light, smooth Chianti is a good substitute.

***CASTAGNE DI MONTE AMIATA:*** Roasted sweet chestnuts are an ideal finish to your hunters' lunch. Purchase a pound of fresh chestnuts to take to your picnic site. With a serrated knife, cut an X through the top of each chestnut and roast them in a metal pan over the fire for thirty to forty minutes. You can also wrap them together in heavy aluminum foil and bury them in the hot ashes for the same amount of time. When they're ready, they will have a soft, creamy texture. Pass the hot chestnuts around and allow your guests to peel their own.

## *Staging the Hunters' Feast*

The hunters' feast is a rustic affair designed especially for fall weather, when chestnuts and porcini are in season. The cooking fire is the center of activity and will provide warmth if there is a chill in the air. Preparing the cookout is a group effort. The hearth must be built, the grill set up, and the fire started. The wine can also be opened now and left to breathe. The quail must be skewered on the spit, roasted, turned, and occasionally basted with olive oil. When the quail is done, the polenta slices are toasted on the hot grill just until they are crusty. Let your guests start with the wild mushroom salad and Italian bread, then serve each guest two wedges of grilled polenta topped with two quail. As you eat, the roasting chestnuts will send their sweet fragrance into the fall air.

## PICTURE CREDITS

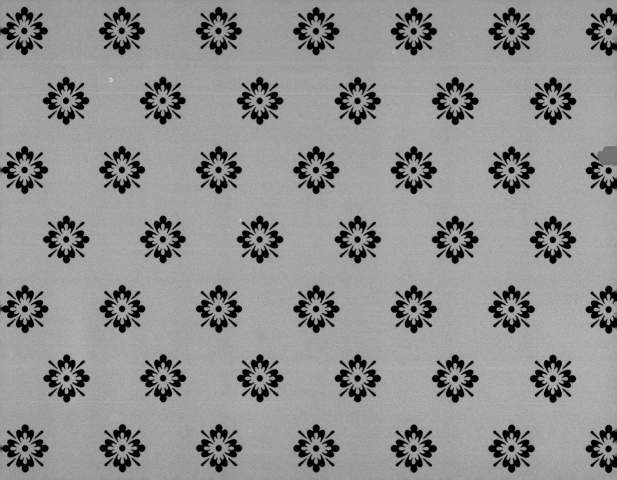

# CARPENTRY

*by* KARIN KELLY  *pictures by* GEORGE OVERLIE

Lerner Publications Company • Minneapolis, Minnesota

LIBRARY OF CONGRESS CATALOGING IN PUBLICATION DATA

Kelly, Karin.
  Carpentry.

  (An Early Craft Book)
  SUMMARY: Introduces the tools and woods suitable for
carpentry projects and gives instructions for making a bookcase and a birdhouse.

  1. Carpentry—Juvenile literature. [1. Carpentry.  2. Wood-
working]  I. Overlie, George, illus.  II. Title.

TH5607.K44                      694                    72-13342
ISBN 0-8225-0857-5

# Contents

# A carpenter's workshop

A carpenter's workshop is a busy place. There are all sorts of interesting things to see, hear, and smell. You can watch the carpenter take plain wooden boards and transform them into beautiful chests, or tables, or chairs. The pounding of his hammer and the hum of his saw make strange, sweet music. The workshop smells good too. The wood has a clean, out-of-doors smell. There are also sharp odors from paints, stains, and turpentine. The activity, noise, and smells make you feel like something exciting is happening in the workshop.

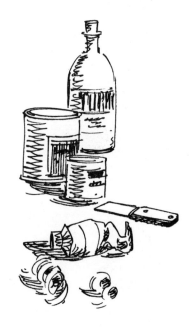

A carpenter's workshop is fun to visit and even more fun to work in. When you learn carpentry in a workshop, you can make lots of noise, work with interesting tools and beautiful materials, and make things that you can use all around your house and yard.

By learning carpentry, you can also become a better problem solver. Carpenters must be able to figure out how to make things that are

strong and well balanced. A good carpenter would not make a tippy table.

At one time, almost everyone knew how to do some simple kinds of carpentry. In early frontier days, the furniture and even the houses were built by the pioneers themselves. The pioneers made houses and pieces of furniture that were meant to serve a function. They did not always have time to make elegant or fancy things. Yet, in the simple carpentry of the pioneers, there is a kind of natural beauty. The wood itself is beautiful, and the simplicity that the rough homes and furniture represent is beautiful too.

Modern homes and furniture look much more "finished" than pioneer homes and furniture. But modern carpenters use the same principles that the pioneer carpenters used. In fact, no matter how complicated a piece of carpentry looks, every corner and angle has been made by skillfully joining two or more pieces of wood together. The more skillful a joiner you become, the more beautiful your carpentry will be.

You will probably not become skillful right away. Good carpenters practice for many years before they become expert enough to make a fine cabinet or a perfectly balanced table. But if you want to learn, you must begin somewhere. And if you choose to make a simple thing, you can make an item that is both good-looking and useful.

## Uses and qualities of wood

To begin, let's learn something about wood. You should know what kinds of woods are best suited for the different kinds of things you will build.

Wood, of course, comes from trees. In the Northern Hemisphere, there are two kinds of trees. There are coniferous (ko-NIF-er-us) trees, or evergreen trees, which keep their needle-like leaves all year round. All kinds of pine trees are coniferous. These trees give us softwood. There are also deciduous (des-SID-you-us) trees, which shed their leaves every fall. Oak, birch, and many other deciduous trees give us hardwood.

*coniferous*

*deciduous*

Softwood is easier to work with than hardwood, so we will take our first steps in carpentry with softwood. When you have learned more about working with wood and tools, you might like to try using hardwood. The things you make from hardwood will last a very long time. They may even have a longer life than you will have.

*annual rings*

There are other things that a carpenter must think about besides the softness or hardness of the wood. For instance, the structure of trees also affects the kinds of things that carpenters can do with wood. When you look at a tree stump or a slice of wood cut crosswise from the center of the tree, you will see that there is a ringed pattern in the wood. The rings are called annual rings. The tree grows larger and adds a new ring annually, or every year.

When trees are cut into logs, and when the logs are sawed into boards, the annual rings show up in a different kind of pattern in the boards. The pattern is called the grain of the board. When a log is simply sawed into strips,

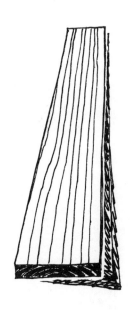

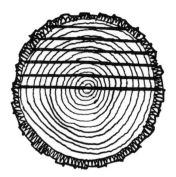

*slash-sawn*

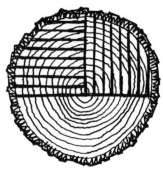

*quarter-sawn*

*3-ply plywood*

the grain appears as wavy lines in the board. This kind of board is called a plain, or slash-sawn, board. It is an inexpensive kind of lumber and quite suitable for the kind of carpentry you will do when you begin.

A more expensive, stronger kind of board is cut from more perfect and valuable trees than those used for slash-sawn boards. It is called quarter-sawn lumber. To make quarter-sawn boards, the log is first cut into quarters. Then the quarters are cut into boards at right angles to the annual rings. The grain in quarter-sawn boards appears as almost straight lines that run from the top to the bottom of the board. When you want to make a finer piece of carpentry, it will be worth your while to buy quarter-sawn lumber.

There is one other kind of lumber you should know about. It is called plywood. Plywood is quite inexpensive and can be used for many beginning projects in carpentry. Plywood is laminated (LAM-in-ate-ted) wood, or thin sheets of wood glued together. Because a sheet of plywood is not a solid board, it sometimes splinters when you try to join it. But if you work carefully, plywood is a very handy material. It can be sawed easily, and you can use large sheets of it to do jobs that would normally require the use of many regular boards.

## Visiting the lumber yard

The best way to learn about different kinds of boards is to visit a lumber yard. There you will see the lumber sizes that are available to you. A lumber man will describe a piece of lumber as a one-inch by ten-inch board. But you must learn that the actual measurements of the board are approximately three-quarters inch by nine-and-one-half inches. And even these measurements do not always hold true. The size of the board depends a great deal upon the sawmill it came from and the type of board-finishing equipment the sawmill used. Board-finishing equipment is not the same in all sawmills.

## Tools

Besides learning about the qualities of lumber, you must also learn how to use carpenters' tools. Tools are fascinating things. They are stronger and tougher than our arms and hands. They help us carry out the brilliant ideas we get about improving and beautifying our lives. If you learn to let tools work for you, you will be able to accomplish many things that you would not be able to do by using only your muscles. A clever child with a tool will be more successful than a giant without one.

When I describe the projects in this book, I will use lumber-yard measurements, and you will have to remember that the boards are actually some fractions of an inch smaller than the measurements given. To see how much they vary from lumber-yard measurements, measure the first boards you buy. As you learn more about carpentry, you will also learn to automatically subtract the fractions of inches.

These tools are essential to any kind of carpentry work:

tape measure

saw

try square

pencil

hammer

nails

rasp

file

sandpaper

|  |  |
|---|---|
| crosscut saw | nails |
| try square | rasp |
| tape measure | file |
| hammer | sandpaper. |

You will also need a work bench.

The basement or utility room is a good place to put a work bench, but you can work in your own room if you clean up when you are finished working and put your tools away neatly. Your work bench can be a sturdy packing case or an old table, but it should be just the right height. If it is too high, you will not be able to reach it and work on it comfortably. I am five feet, six inches tall, and my workbench is 32 inches high. If you are eight years old and about average height, you might like a work bench that is about 25 or 27 inches high. You can saw the legs off an old table to make a work bench.

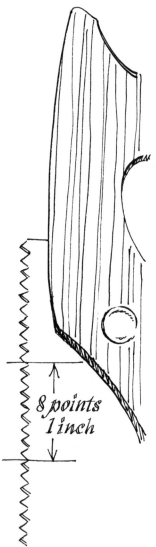

**8 points 1 inch**

# Saw and try square

Let's begin to work with tools by learning how to use a saw. There are many different kinds of saws. Some are large and are meant to cut logs. Some are very thin and fine and are used to cut fancy patterns and holes in wood. Today, many home saws are electric, but they are expensive and somewhat dangerous for a beginning carpenter to use. You should get a sturdy hand saw. One that can be used to do almost all of the sawing you will do at the start is an eight-point crosscut saw. Eight points means that there are eight saw teeth to every inch of saw blade.

Crosscut saws come in two standard lengths —18 inches and 26 inches. You might think that the 18-inch saw looks like it would be easier to handle, but once you learn how to use a saw, you will be happier with the longer blade. An 18-inch saw takes more muscle to work with.

A crosscut saw will cut across the grain of a regular board. If you need to cut into the length of a board, you have to use a rip saw. A rip saw is difficult to handle, so you should buy lumber that does not have to be cut to size "the long way," or "with the grain."

Practice sawing before you begin a project. Get several pieces of scrap lumber. If they are about three feet long, you should be able to handle them easily. A carpenter with lots of tools uses saw horses when he saws, but if you do not have saw horses, you can use two chairs or orange crates to hold the boards you saw. If you are going to saw a piece from a three-foot board, put the board on top of the saw horses, chairs, or crates so that the piece you will be sawing off is balanced between the two supports. Now you can use the try square to draw the line for your saw cut.

A try square is a metal ruler with a metal or wooden handle at one end. The handle is fastened at a right angle to the ruler. When you want to draw a straight line across a board for a saw cut, hold the handle of the try square

*saw horse*

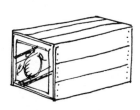

*orange crate
saw horse*

firmly against the side of the board. The right angle formed by the handle and the ruler will permit you to draw a perfectly straight line across the board to guide you as you saw.

*mark all four sides*

When you have set up your sawing platform and have drawn the line for your saw cut, you may begin to saw. Remember to let the tool do the work for you. Put your left knee on top of the board to the left of your pencil line. Grasp the board at the edge in front of your knee. (If you are left-handed, you will use your right hand and knee to keep the board steady.) Then pull the saw teeth up the edge of the board at the pencil line. Push the saw down and pull it up again. It is the downward stroke of the saw that makes the cut. Use the full length of the saw if you can, and don't try to force it to cut.

If you are patient and careful, the saw will cut the board and you will only have to pull it up and push it down. Keep your eye on the pencil line as you saw. Make sure that your cut is straight and true. When you have sawed through most of the board, support the board firmly with your hand until the cut is complete. Boards sometimes splinter and cuts get jagged if the carpenter gets careless when he comes to the end of the cut.

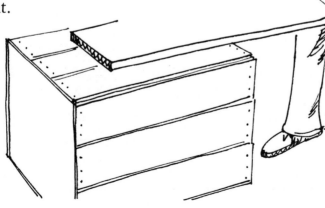

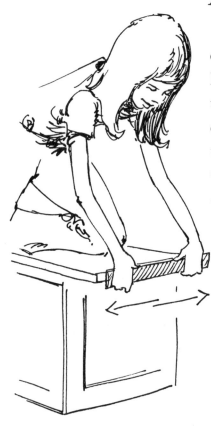

## Rasp, file, and sandpaper

When you have sawed through the board, you can practice using the rasp and file. If you get a half-round rasp, you can use it to add decorative touches to your finished carpentry as well as to do simple finishing work. You will notice that the rasp has much rougher edges than the file. One side of the rasp is also rougher than the other.

### use even pressure

To smooth the ends of a board, hold it so that the end extends beyond the edge of the work bench. Begin finishing the saw cuts by shaving off the roughest edges with the roughest side of the rasp. As the edge of the cut gets smoother, use the finer edge of the rasp. To make the cut as smooth as your skin, use the file and perhaps a final touch-up with fine sandpaper.

18

## Hammer and nails

The next important tool you must learn to use is a hammer. Get a good, sturdy claw hammer that is comfortable for you to lift and swing. You might be comfortable with a 12-ounce hammer. Any size hammer from 12 to 16 ounces will be useful to you, but your choice should depend upon your own strength. A hammer that is too light will not drive nails in very quickly or surely, but a hammer that is too heavy will tire your arms.

Let's learn how to drive nails with a hammer. Practice by nailing two pieces of one-inch board together with one-and-one-half-inch nails. The easiest nails to work with are nails with heads. They are easier to hit with a hammer. Nails without heads are called finishing nails. You can use them when you are very good at driving nails.

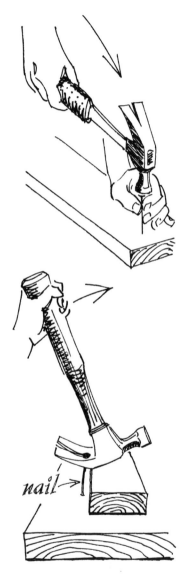

To drive a nail, place it in position on the top board. Grasp the hammer close to the end of the handle; if you do this, you will have more power when you swing it. Hold the nail between your fingers and thumb and gently tap the head of the nail several times until it sticks in the wood. When the nail is stuck, take your fingers away and drive the nail all of the way into the boards. Practice with at least 10 or 12 nails until your aim gets very good. You should drive the nails in very straight. If you try to drive in a bent nail, you will ruin your carpentry. If you should bend a nail, take it out with the hammer claw.

When you need to remove a nail from a board, pound it up from the bottom side of the board until you can insert the claw of the hammer underneath the head of the nail on top. Then put a thin piece of wood under the hammer head and pull the nail out with the claw. The wood under the head of the hammer will prevent it from denting the surface of the board.

*nail*

## A bookcase

When you think you have learned as much as you can about using your tools on wood, you may begin to make your first carpentry project. Let's make a bookcase. It is very easy, and you can put many things besides books in it. You can put your rock collection on part of a shelf; you can use your bookcase to display small sculptures you have made.

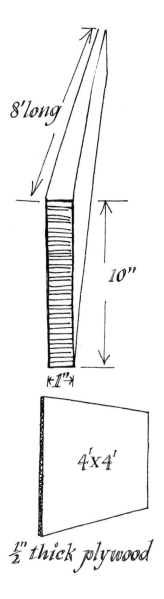

8'long

10"

← 1" →

4'x4'

½" thick plywood

Before we begin to select lumber and make plans, let's learn to write the symbols carpenters use when they write about the sizes of the things they work with. When carpenters write about the lengths and thicknesses of the boards they are using, they do not write out the words "inches" or "feet." They use the symbols " for inches and ' for feet. They also use the symbol *x* for "by." A piece of board 12 inches square and one inch thick would be called a 1" *x* 12" *x* 12" piece of board. If the board were three feet long, it would be called a 3' board.

Now you can get your lumber for the bookcase. Buy an 8' length of 1" *x* 10" pine board. To make your bookcase stronger, buy a piece of 1/2" plywood. If you would like to have the plywood on hand for other projects, buy a 4' *x* 4' square piece. You can cut the piece you need from the large square. You can also buy some pre-cut decorative molding for your bookcase. If you see some that you like at the lumber yard, buy at least 2' of it. You can buy 1-1/2" finishing nails, 1" wood screws, and wood glue at the lumber yard too. You can use these materials for several different projects, and it will save time if you have them on hand.

When you have the lumber and other materials you need, you can plan and measure the wood for your bookcase. It will have two side supports and two shelves. Both supports and shelves will be cut from the 8' board. If you make the side supports 27" high and the shelves 21" long, you will have just enough lumber in the 8' board.

If you saw the 8' board exactly in half, you will have two shorter (4') boards that will be easier to handle. Each half will provide one side support for the bookcase and one shelf. But before you begin, be absolutely certain that your long board is exactly 8' long. This is one project where you will not have any scrap lumber left.

Take one of the 4' boards and, using a yardstick, measure off 27" and mark the board with a pencil at that point on one edge of the board.

2'

decorative molding

1½" finishing nails

1" wood screws

wood glue

*measure, mark, and cut two 4' boards*

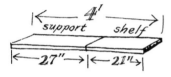

*mark with square and cut*

*use rasp and file on all raw edges*

*sand all boards with fine sandpaper*

Then use the try square to draw a perfectly straight line across the board at that point.

When you have drawn the line, put the board between saw horses or chairs as you did when you practiced sawing. Then saw the board in two pieces as perfectly as you can. Measure, mark, and saw the other 4' length of board. Now you have both supports and shelves. Finish the raw edges of the saw cuts carefully with rasp, file, and sandpaper. Sand the top and bottom of the boards clean with fine sandpaper too. Be sure to sand with the grain, that is, up and down the length of the board. If you try to sand across the grain, you will scratch and ruin the wood. When the boards are smooth, you may begin to put the bookcase together.

If you bought some pre-carved molding, you may attach it to the shelves before you join them to the side pieces. You can attach the molding with white wood glue and nails. Measure and saw off two pieces of molding that are exactly the length of the bookcase shelves (21"). File and sand the ends of the pieces. The molding can serve as a kind of railing on the top edge of the shelf, or it can simply be used as decoration that extends from the bottom edge of the shelf. Glue the molding in place just under the edge of the shelf pieces. Then reinforce the glue by driving 1-1/2" finishing nails into the shelf board and molding.

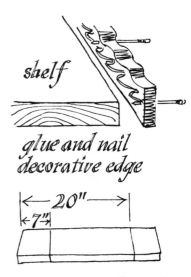

shelf

glue and nail
decorative edge

←—20"—→
←7"→

measure and mark
both support pieces

Now you may join the shelves and sides. You can make two really useful shelves if you join them to the supports about 12" apart. Lay the yardstick on one support piece, and make a pencil mark at the 7" point and at the 20" point. These points are the places where the shelves will be joined.

Use your work bench to prop up the boards as you nail them together. Thick books or scrap lumber will support the shelf board so that it is upright and even with the top of the work bench. Lay the support piece on top of the shelf board at one of the pencil points. Line the boards up perfectly on both sides. Nail them together firmly.

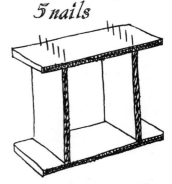

5 nails

turn over and
nail

setting nails

fill holes with
plastic wood

cut plywood and
nail to back of
bookcase

You should use at least five 1-1/2" finishing nails for each shelf joining. Drive the nails in straight and true. If you would like to hide the nails on the finished bookcase, drive them even further into the wood with a tool called a nail set, and cover them with plastic wood. When the plastic wood is dry, you can sand it down and the nails will be hidden forever.

After you have nailed on the second shelf, you are ready to attach the other support piece. You will not need to support the shelves on the bench when you attach this piece. Nail the shelves in place carefully, sink the nails, and stand your bookcase upright. To make your bookcase stand steady, measure and saw out a square of plywood that is as large as the entire back of the bookcase. Finish and sand the edges of the plywood, and nail it to the back of the bookcase as neatly as you can. You do not need to sink these nails because they will not show.

When your bookcase is completely assembled, you may stain it or paint it. I like wood stains on pieces of furniture like bookcases. You can stain your pine bookcase with a variety of wood colorings. You can stain it so that it looks like a light-colored wood or a dark-colored wood. Apply the stain with a cloth and let it dry thoroughly. You might also want to use shellac or varnish to make a glazed, or shiny, finish on the bookcase. You can buy shellac or varnish in a spray can, or you can paint it on with a brush. Be sure that you let it dry completely before you touch the surface of the wood.

*stain and varnish*

## A birdhouse

Are you ready for a more complicated carpentry project? I think you are. Let's make a birdhouse. Children have been making birdhouses for a long time. I still like to make birdhouses and hang them in my yard. The families of birds that live in my yard every summer are dear neighbors and friends. Their songs are the delight of my summer mornings.

**27**

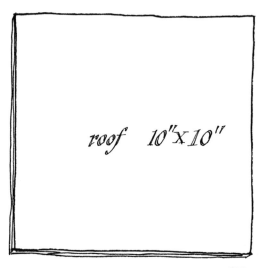

roof 10"X10"

floor 8"x8"

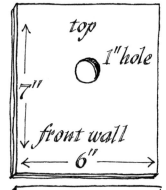

top

1" hole

7"

front wall

6"

back wall
6"X6"

We can make a simple birdhouse from ply-wood. When you have learned how to put pieces together very well, you can make one out of regular 1/2" boards. Our birdhouse will be very easy to make. It will have a slanting roof, four walls, and a floor. It will have a round door and a perch outside for the birds to sit on.

First we must decide how large the birdhouse will be. Let's make a home for Jenny Wren. We need six pieces of plywood for the wren house and one 6" x 1/4" dowel for the perch. Measure and saw out the following pieces of plywood:

One 6"-square piece for the back wall
one 6" x 7" piece for the front wall

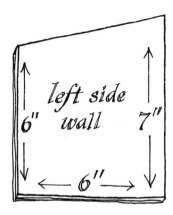

left side wall
6" 7"
← 6" →

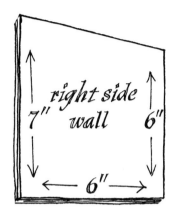

right side wall
7" 6"
← 6" →

6" x ¼"
dowel for perch

1" finishing nails

1½" wood screws

hook and bolt

two pieces with slanted tops for the sides. (Measure and draw lines in the shape of an open-ended "square" on the plywood. The lines should be 6" long on one side and the bottom, and 7" long on the third side. Use a ruler and connect the top of the 6" side to the top of the 7" side.)

one 10"-square piece for the roof

one 8"-square piece for the floor.

You will also need:

a package of 1" finishing nails

a package of wood screws

a hook with a bolt.

*cut and sand all pieces*

drill 1" hole...

...and ¼" hole

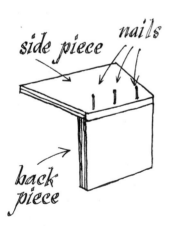

side piece

nails

back piece

When the pieces are cut, file and sand all of the edges until they are smooth. Now you must find a friend with a drill and a 1" bit to drill a hole in the front piece to use as a door. Ask your friend to drill another 1/4" hole just under the door for the perch. Sand the edges smooth around the holes.

You should also attach the bolted hook to the center of the roof piece at this point. Drill one more hole, screw in the hook, and secure it with a nut on the underside of the roof piece.

Now you can put the wren house together. Join the back piece to one of the sides with 1" finishing nails. Use at least three nails per joining. Join the other side to the back and the front to the sides. Then lay the roof on top of the walls and measure its position so that the overhanging part of the roof is even on all sides. Mark the underside of the roof with a pencil, and use these marks as a guide when you nail the roof on. When you have finished the roof, you can attach the floor.

You should attach the floor with wood screws so that you can take it off in the fall and clean the birdhouse. Measure and mark the floor so that the house sits on it evenly. To use screws for joining, you must make a "starter" hole to put the screws into. It would be very hard work to put a screw in solid wood. To make the starter hole, drive a 1-1/2" nail through both floor and side pieces. Don't drive it all the way in, but just far enough to puncture the side board. Then pull the nail out with the hammer claw. Now you can simply put the screw in with a screw driver. Screw it in firmly. Use at least eight screws to fasten the floor of the wren house. Drive the dowel into the hole under the door with a hammer.

Paint the birdhouse if you like. It's fun to paint. Use house paint on the sides, floor, and roof. You might also like to decorate the house with painted designs. Use acrylic paint for the designs. Make a patriotic birdhouse with red, white, and blue paint.

*nail on the remaining side and the front,*

*then nail on the roof with equal overhang on all sides.*

*screw on bottom*

Your birdhouse is finished! You can hang it with a rope or chain from a tree in your yard, and wait for Jenny Wren to come home for the summer.

While you're waiting, why not try some other carpentry projects that you can design for yourself. Make a bookcase with three or four shelves. Make a covered box with hinges for toys, books, or clothes. Make a footstool. Make a sturdy shelf for your workshop. Don't be afraid to experiment, and you will learn by doing. That is the best way of all to learn.